summer daddy

Your fitness is 100% mental…

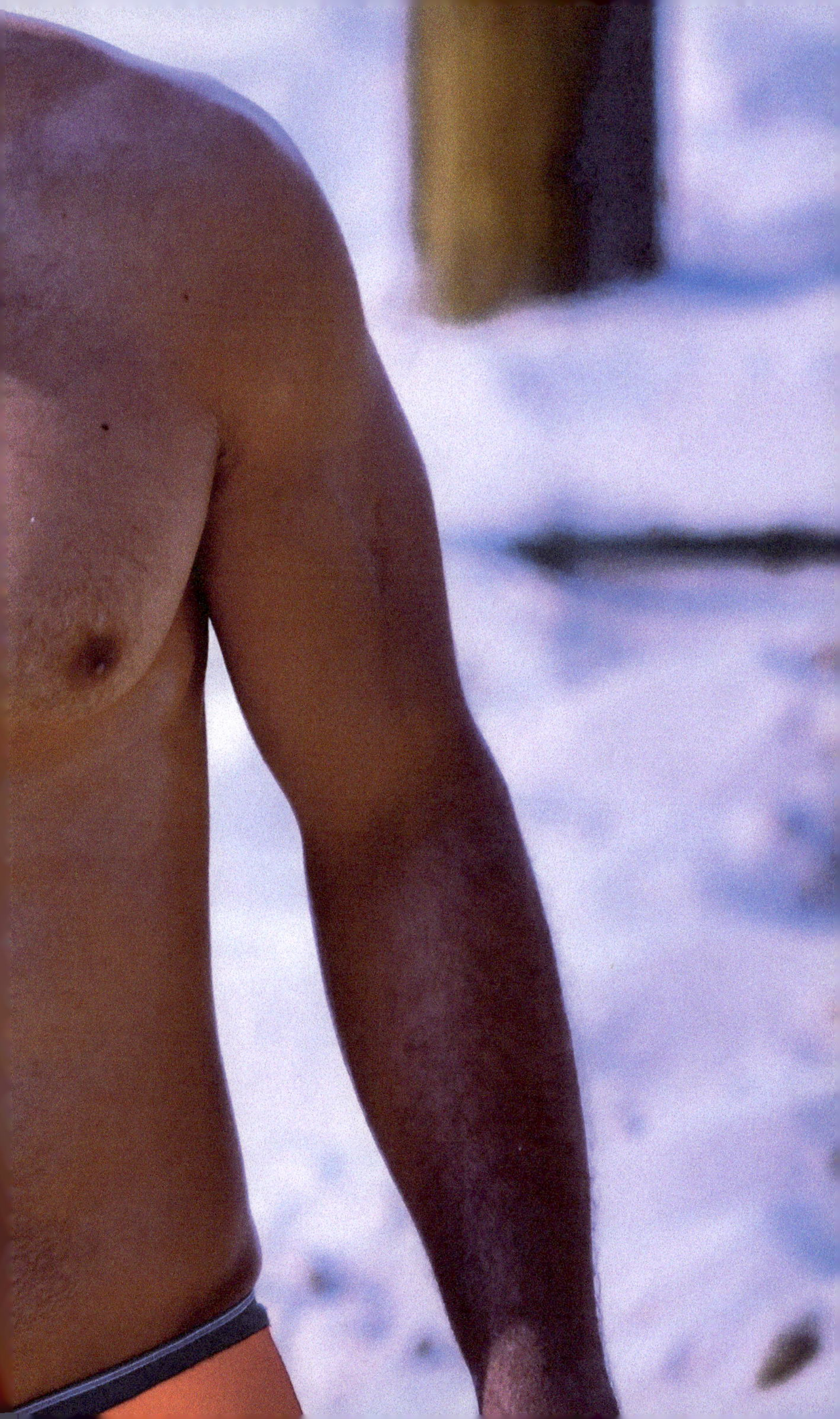

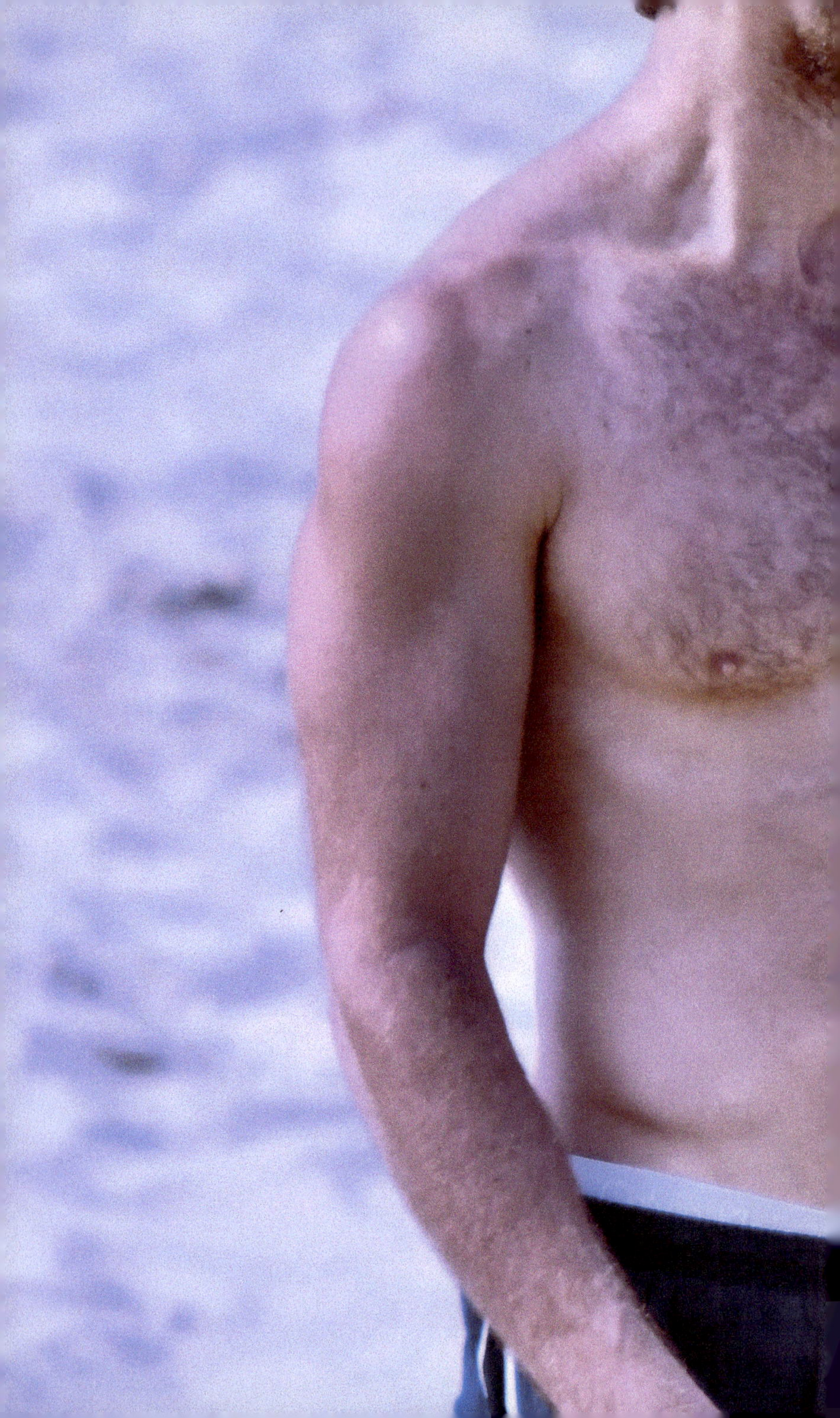

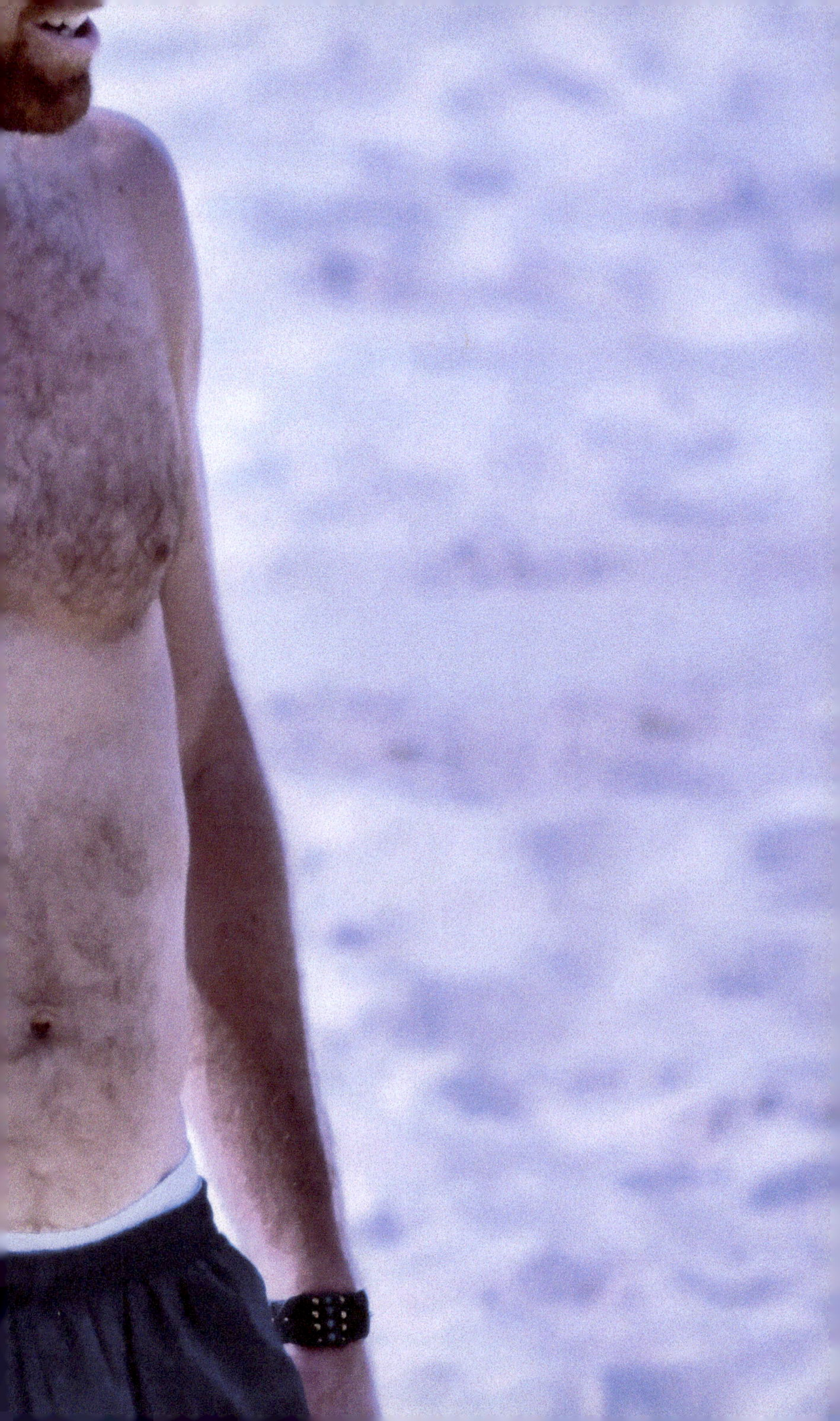

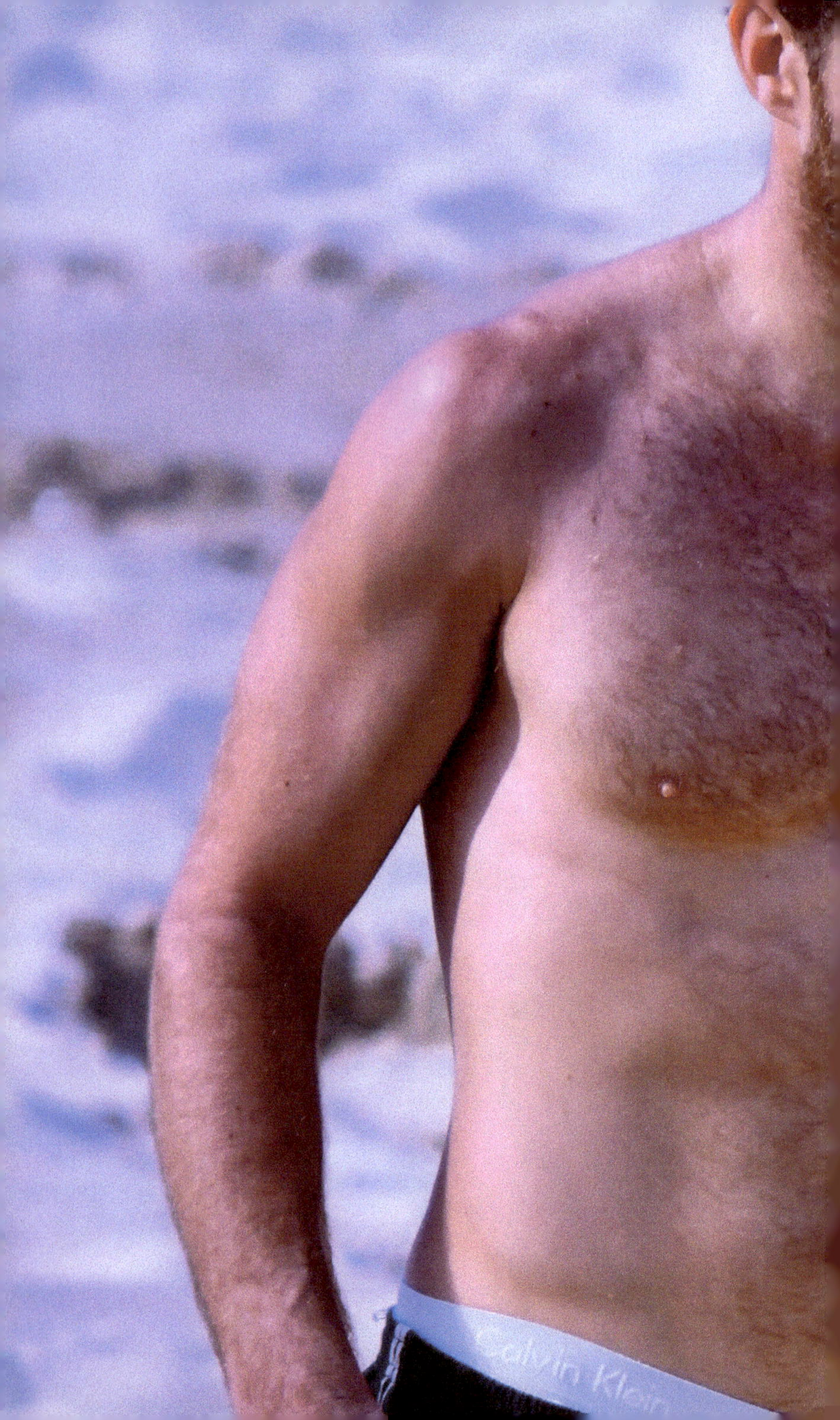
Calvin Klei

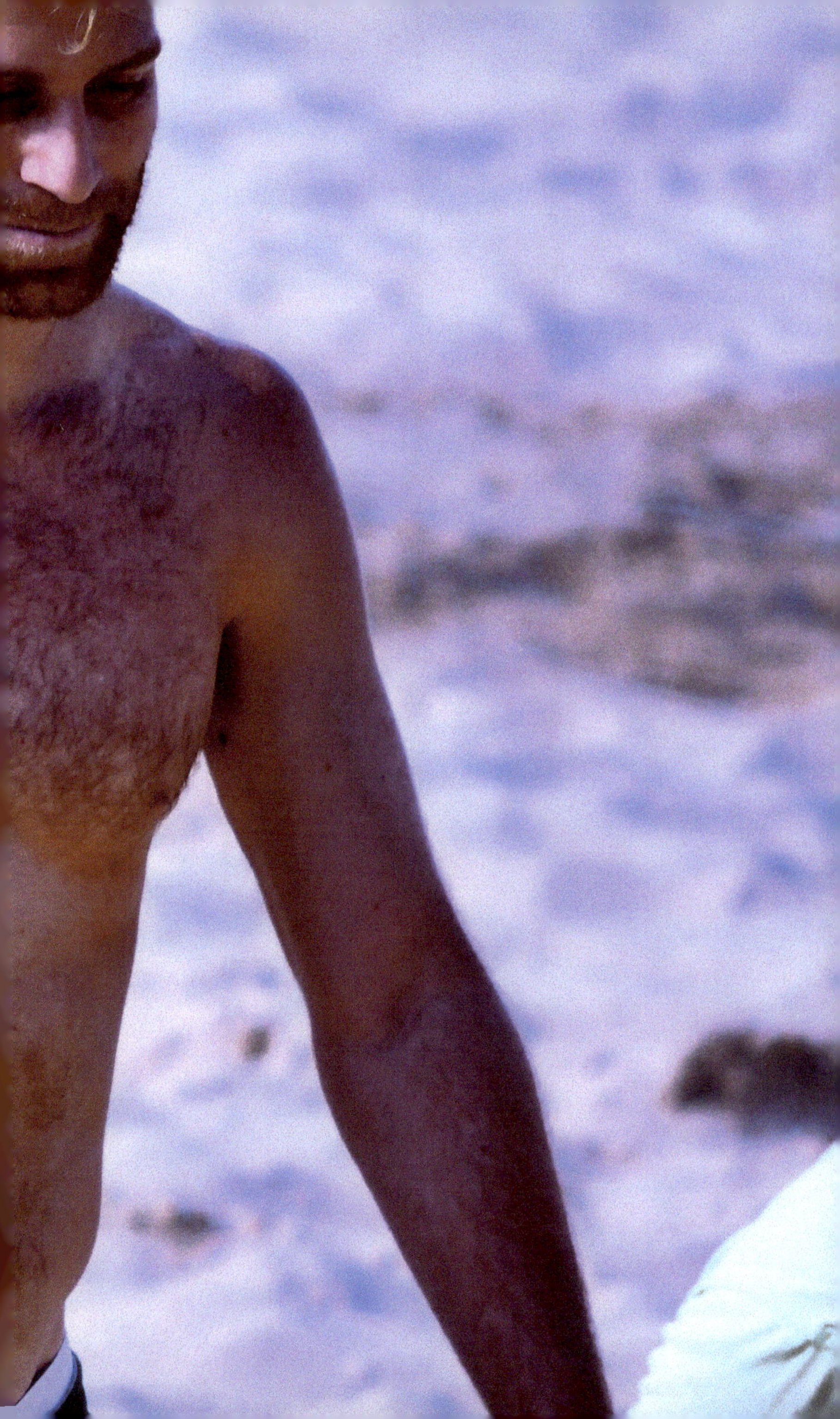

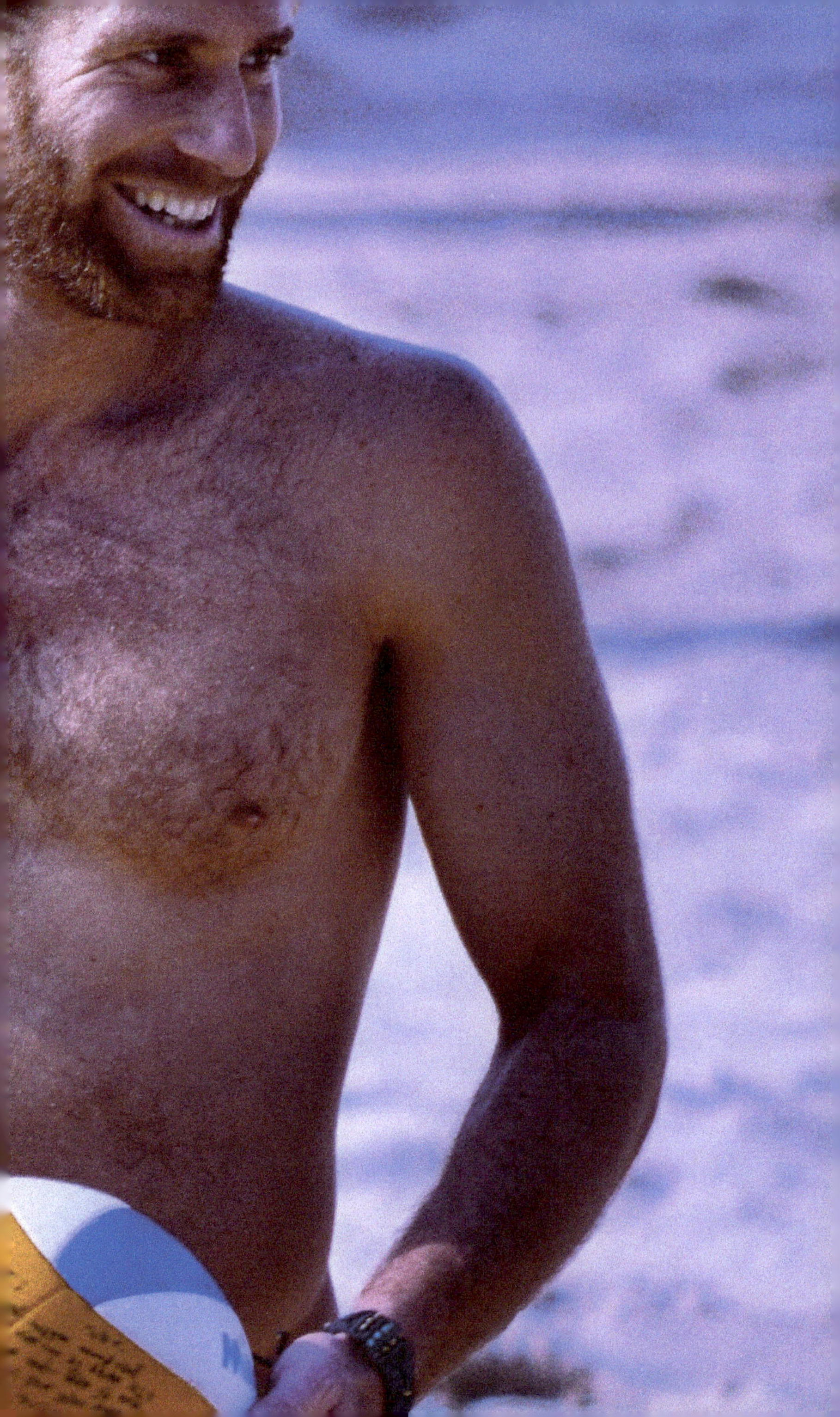

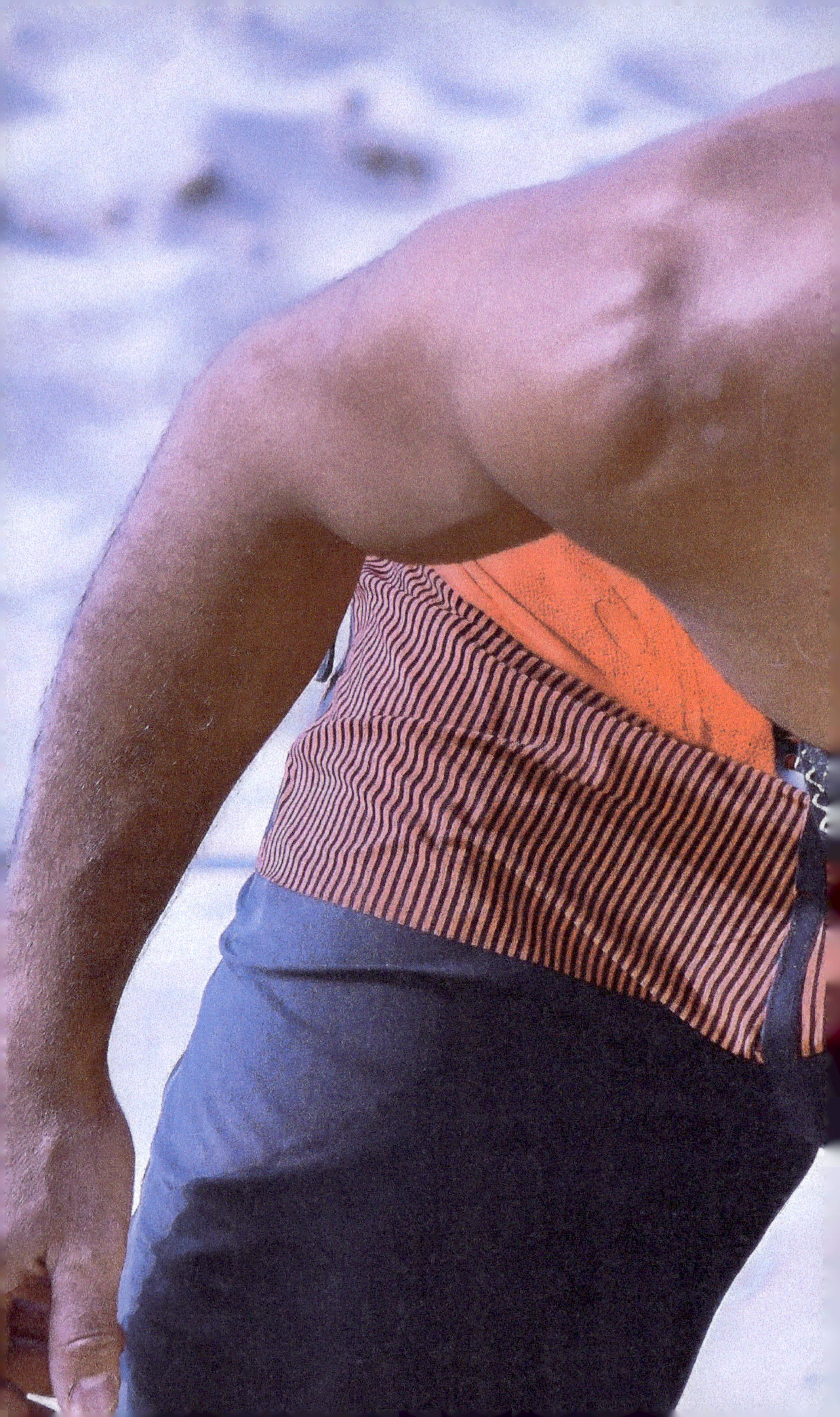

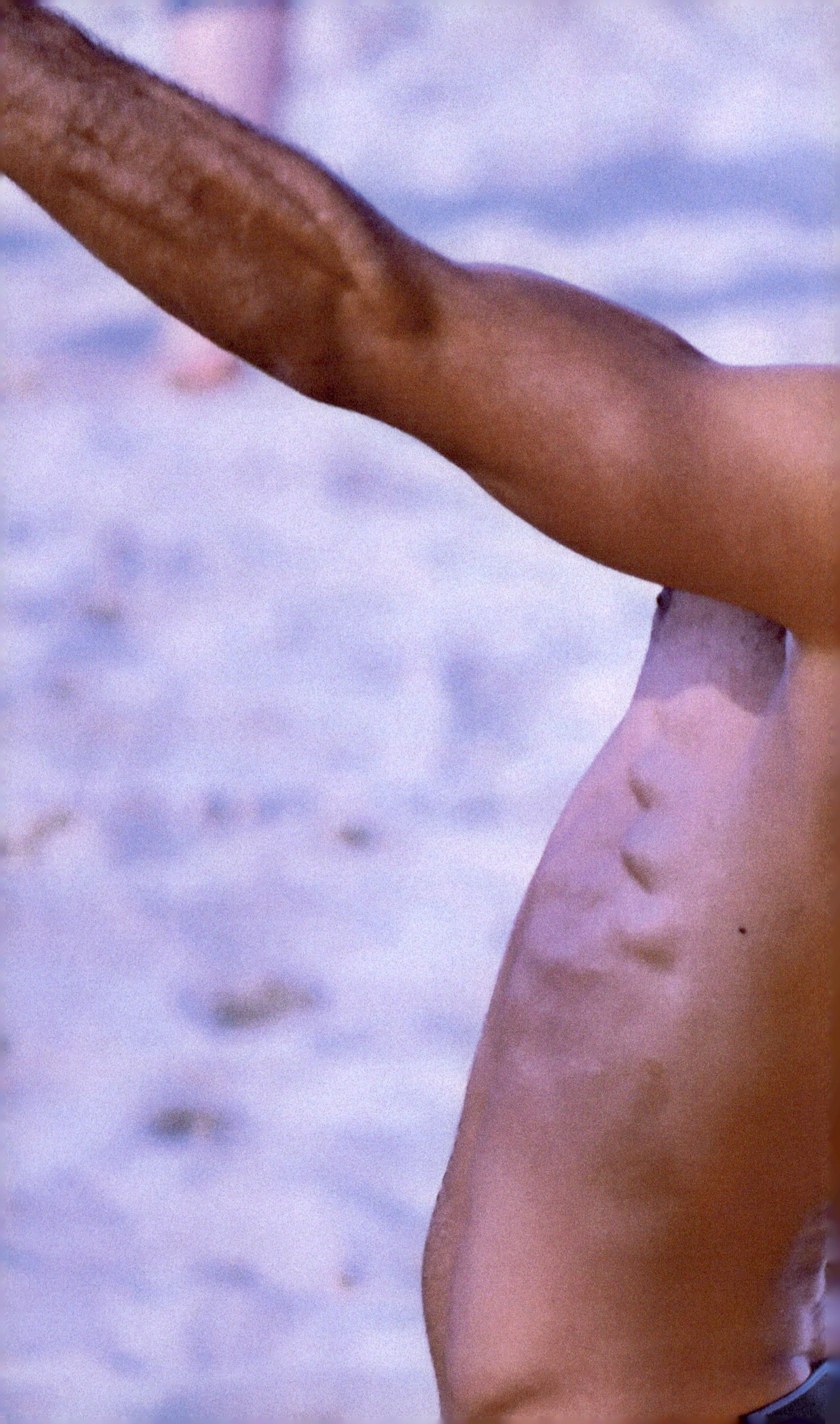

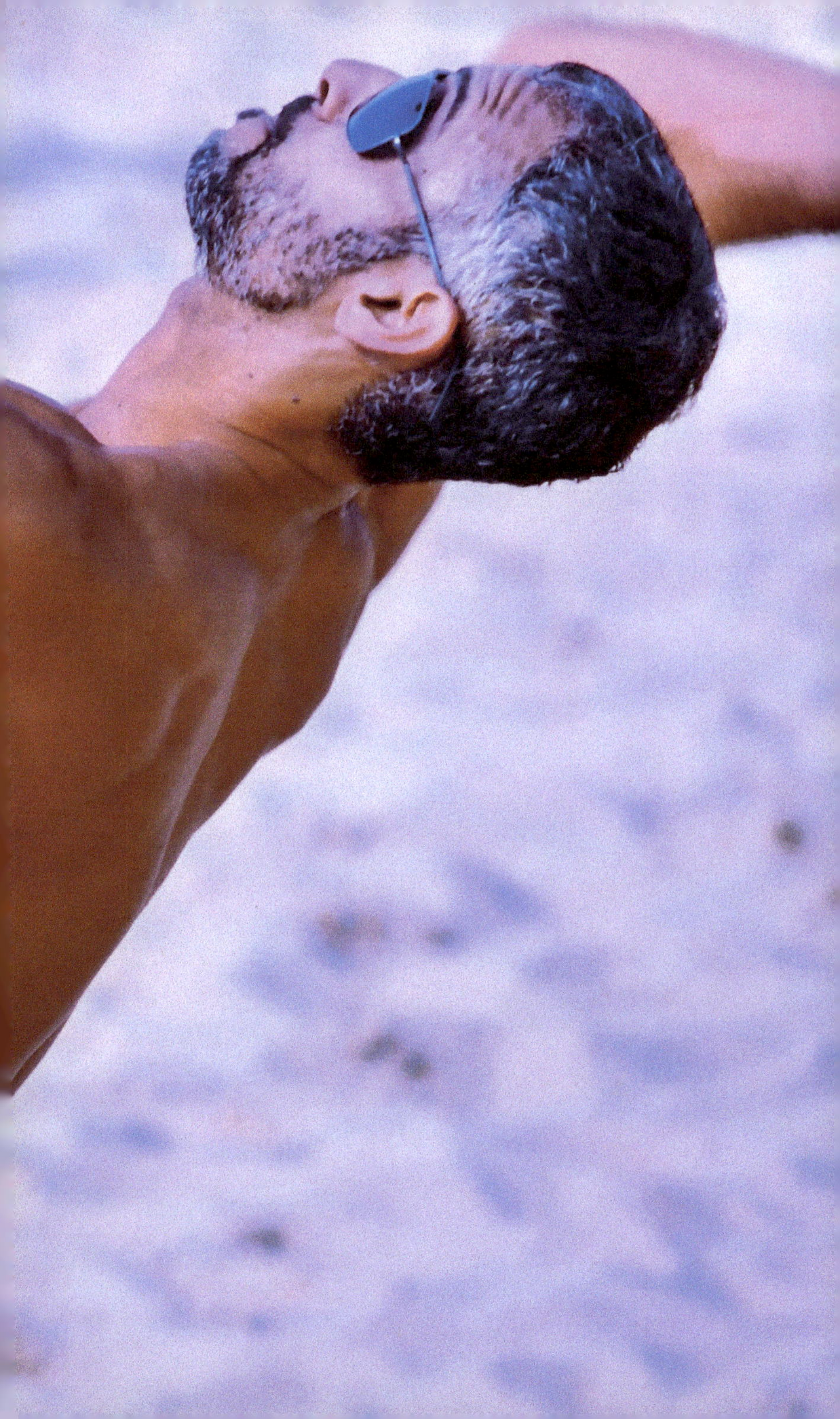

FIVB

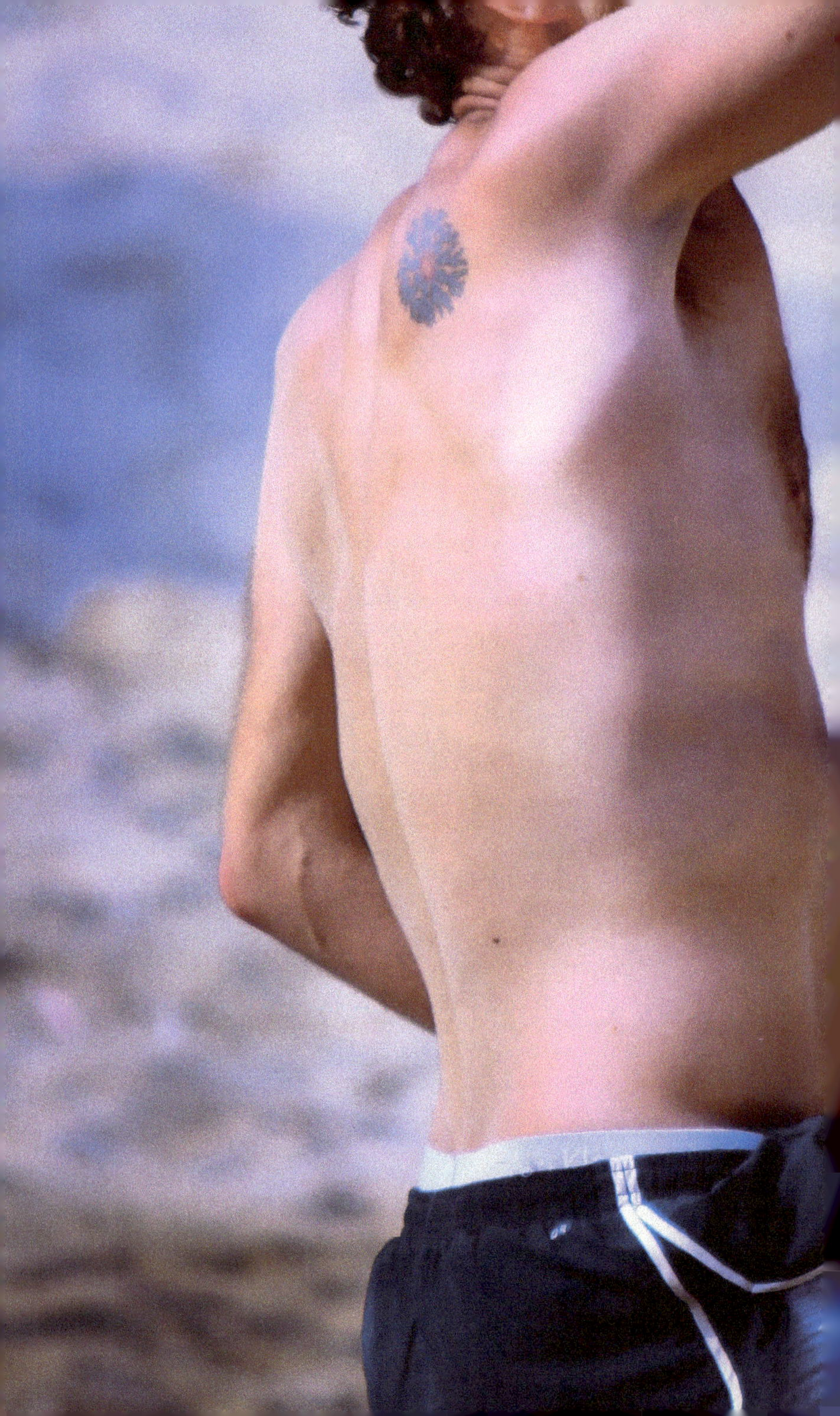

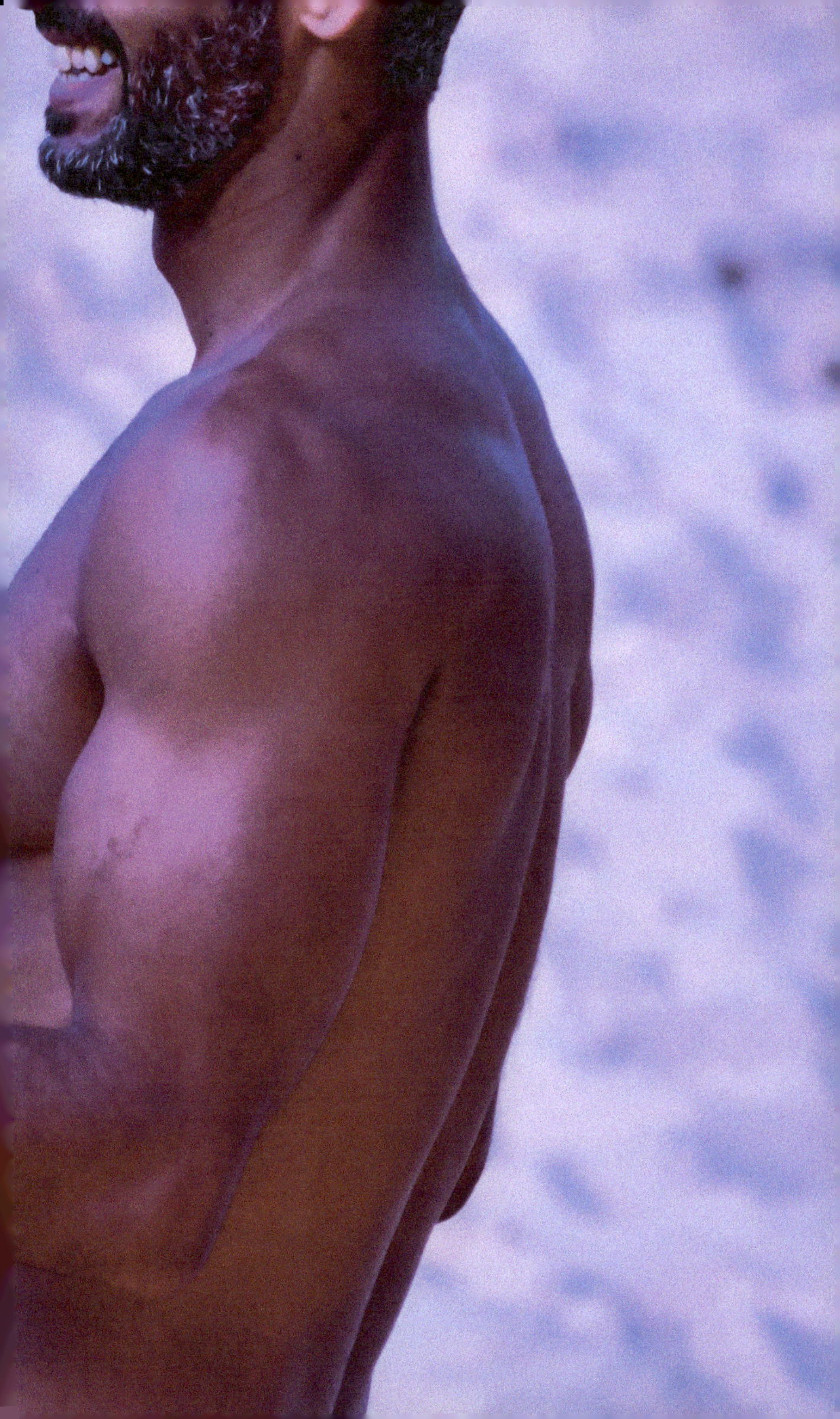

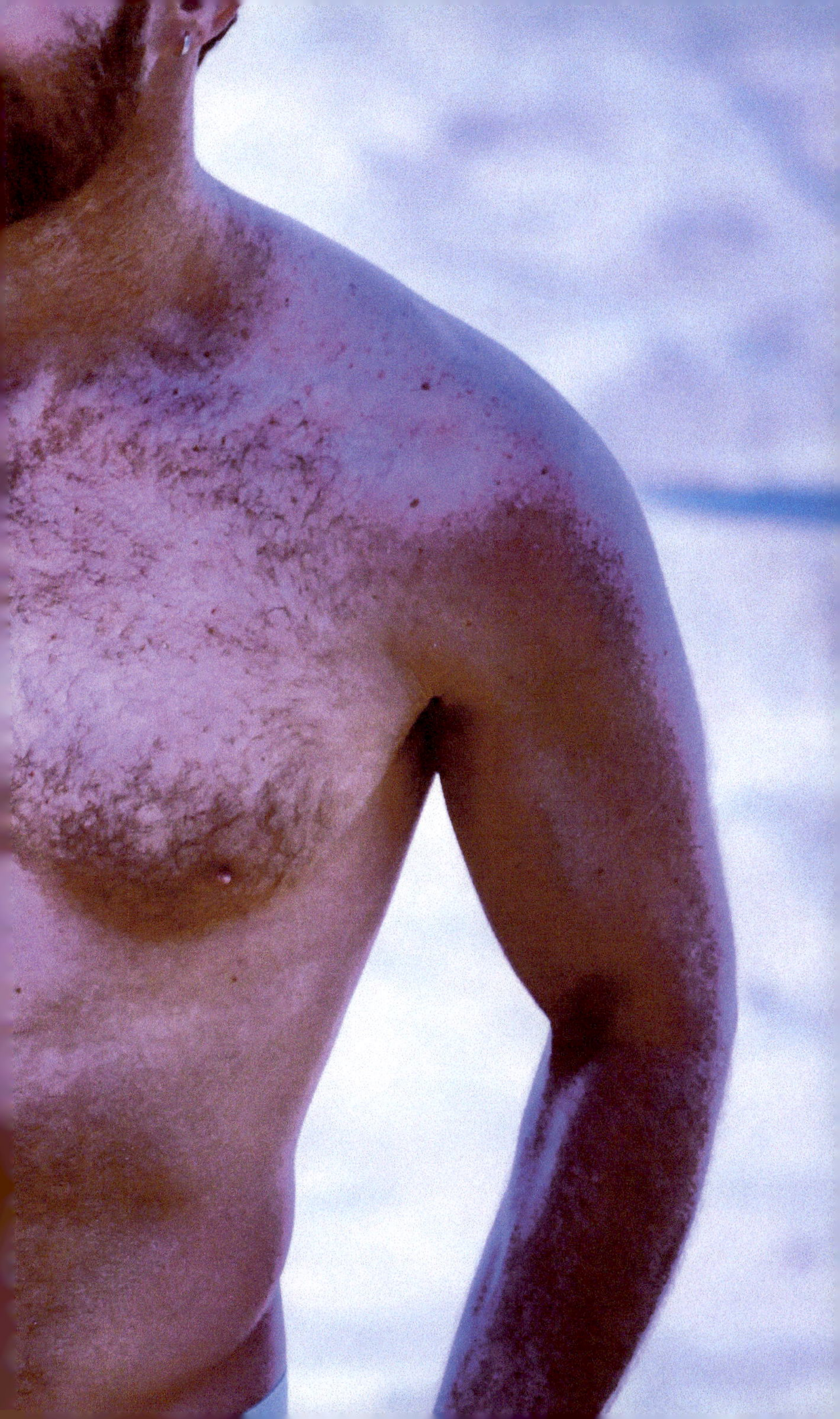

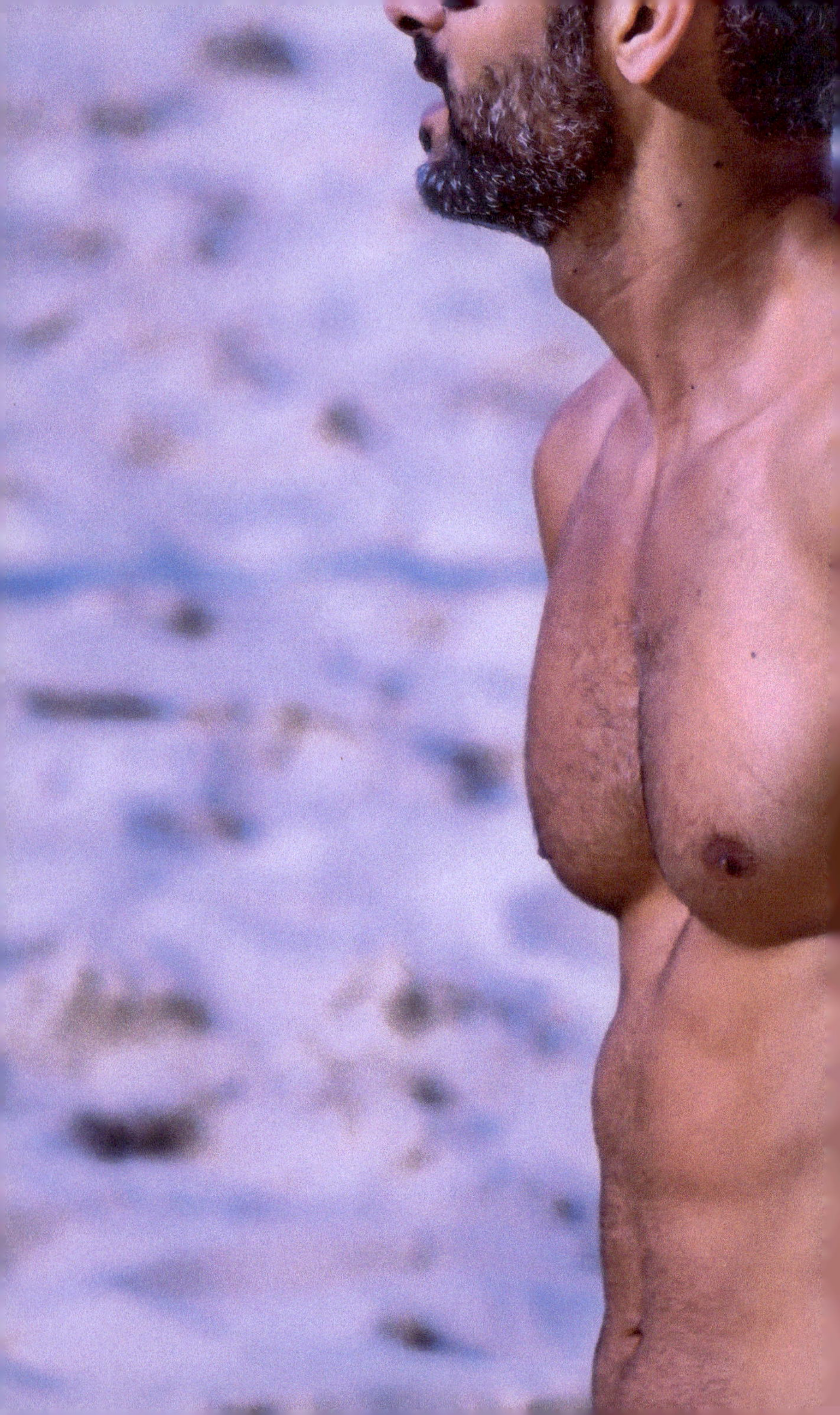

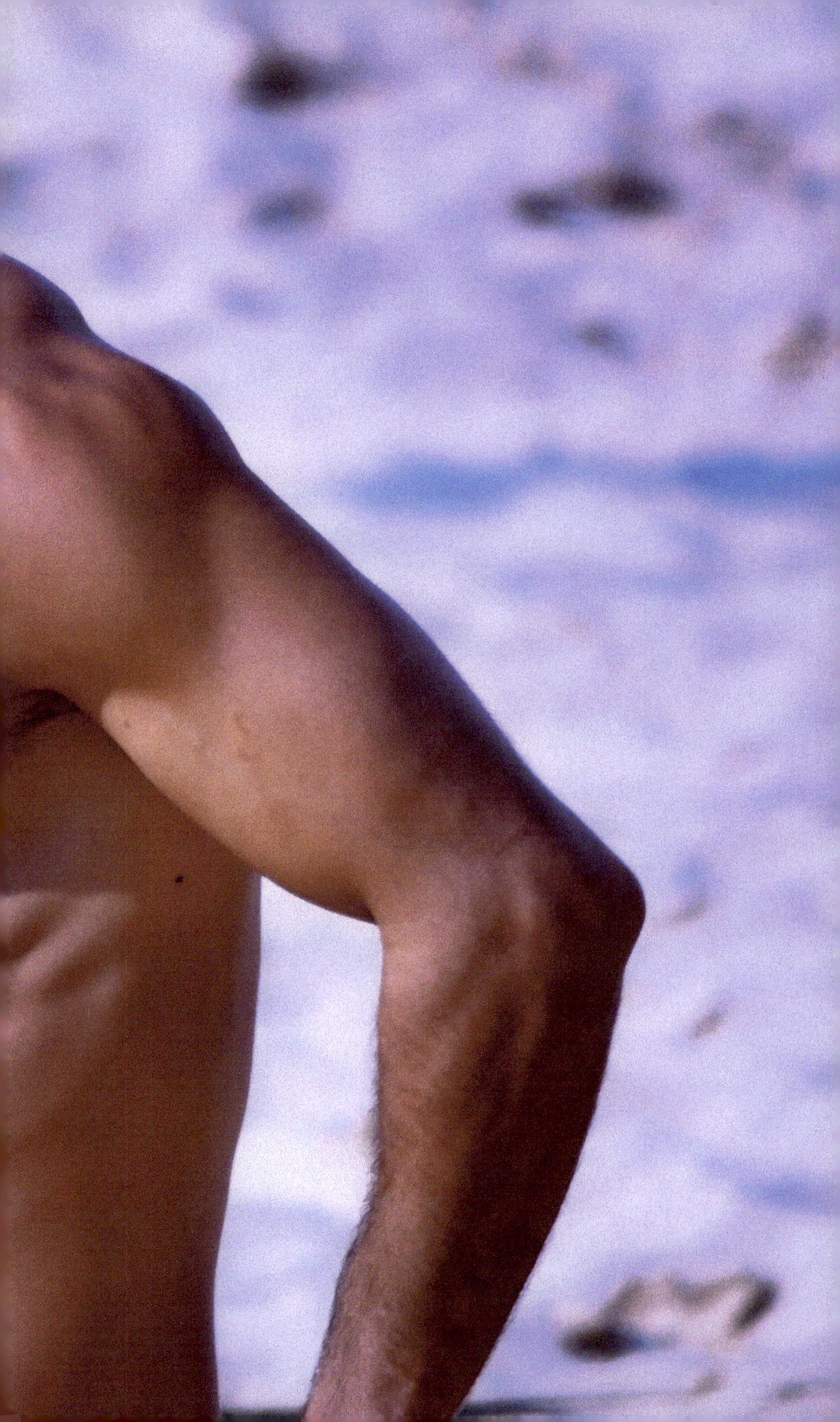

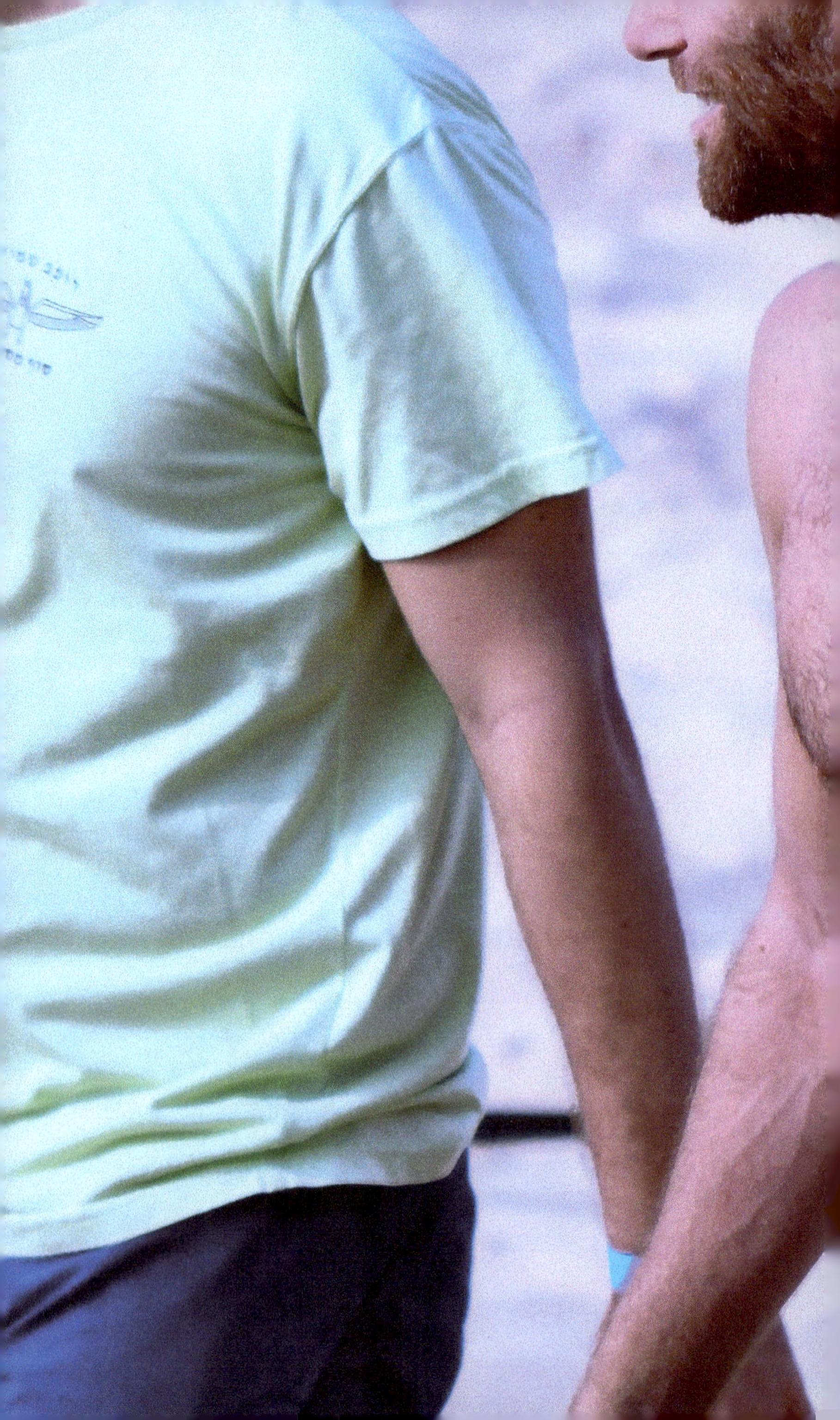

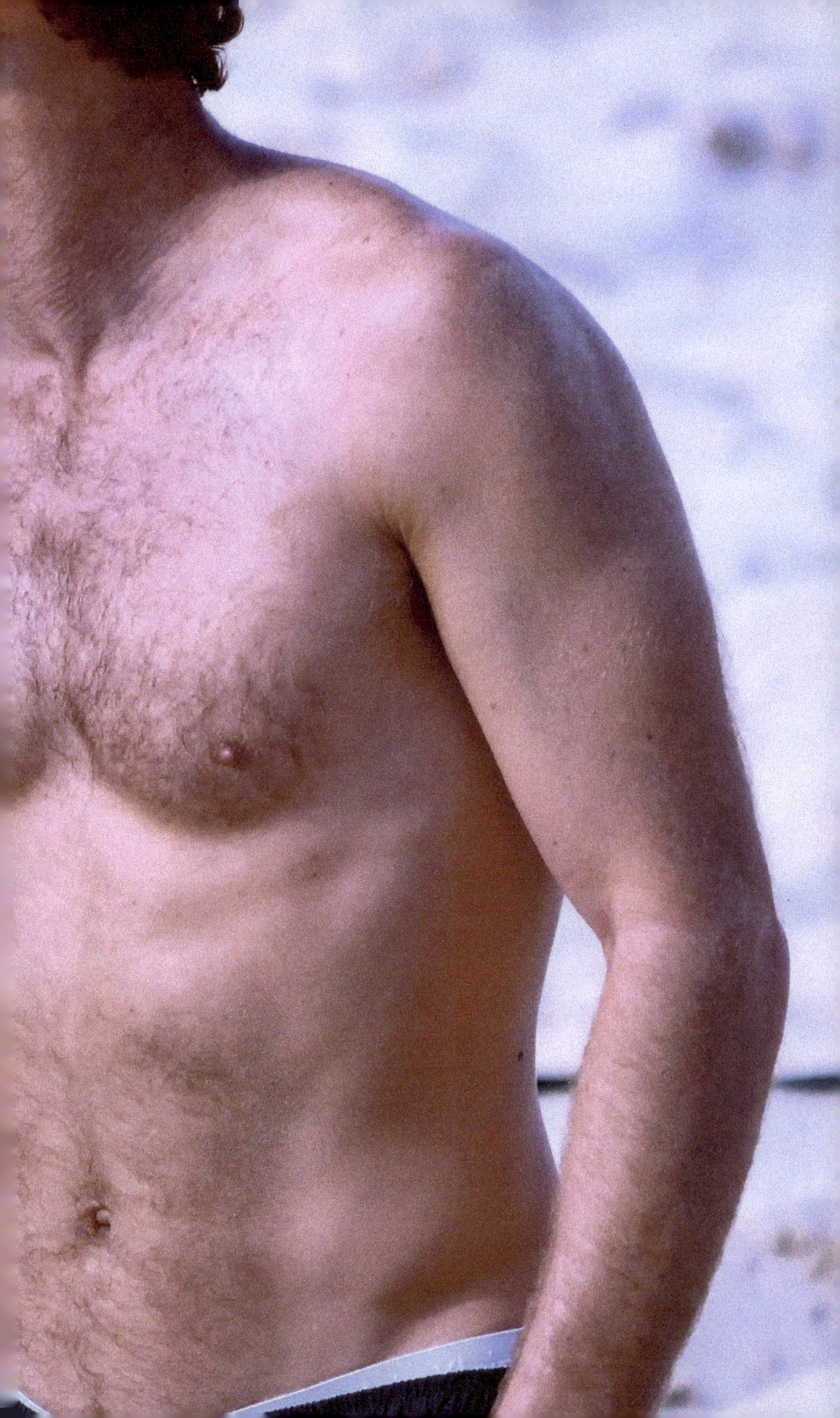